SNOWBOARDING
FOR FUN!

D1544422

By Beth Gruber

Content Adviser: Amy Ohran, Snowboarding Director, Mt. Bachelor, Oregon
Reading Adviser: Frances J. Bonacci, Reading Specialist, Cambridge, Massachusetts

COMPASS POINT BOOKS

MINNEAPOLIS, MINNESOTA

Compass Point Books
3109 West 50th Street, #115
Minneapolis, MN 55410

Visit Compass Point Books on the Internet at *www.compasspointbooks.com*
or e-mail your request to *custserv@compasspointbooks.com*

Photographs ©: Mike Brinson/Getty Images, front cover (left); Ron Leighton, front cover (right), back cover; Corel, front cover (background), 4 (bottom left), 5, 47; Getty Royalty Free, 4 (center), 8–9, 9, 22–23, 26–27, 28–29, 42 (bottom left), 43 (top & bottom), 44 (right); Image 100, 4 (bottom right); Photos.com, 6–7, 7, 21; Ingram Publishing, 10–11; courtesy of Burton, 11 (top), 11 (center top), 11 (bottom); PhotoSpin, 11 (center); Corbis Royalty Free, 13, 32–33; Steven E. Frischling/Getty Images, 14–15; Elsa Hasch/Getty Images, 17; Agence Zoom/Getty Images, 18–19, 45; Jamie Squire/Getty Images, 25; Donald Miralle/Getty Images, 31, 35; Jed Jacobsohn/Getty Images, 37; Donald Miralle/Getty Images, 38–39; Bud Fawcett/Palmer Snowboards, 40; Brian Bahr/Getty Images, 41; Arttoday, 42 (top left & center); Elsa/Getty Images, 44 (bottom).

Editor: Elizabeth Bond/Bill SMITH STUDIO
Photo Researchers: Sandra Will, Sean Livingstone, and Christie Silver/Bill SMITH STUDIO
Designer: Colleen Sweet/Bill SMITH STUDIO

Library of Congress Cataloging-in-Publication Data
Gruber, Beth.
Snowboarding for fun! / by Beth Gruber.
p. cm. — (Sports for fun!)
Includes bibliographical references and index.
ISBN 0-7565-0489-9 (hardcover: alk. paper)
1. Snowboarding. I. Title. II. Series.
GV857.S57G78 2004
796.93'9–dc21   2003006675

Table of Contents

Ground Rules

Ready, Set, Go

People, Places, and Fun

Note: In this book, there are two kinds of vocabulary words. *Snowboarding Words to Know* are words specific to snowboarding. They are in **bold** and are defined on page 46. *Other Words to Know* are helpful words that aren't related only to snowboarding. They are in ***bold and italicized.*** These are defined on page 47.

The New Kid on the Block

In the sports world, snowboarding is the new kid on the block. It has only been around for about 35 years, but snowboarding has a lot in common with other sports, like surfing, skiing, and skateboarding. The sport developed from many different people's ideas. Each person borrowed from sports they knew to create a new, exciting sport!

In 1965, Sherman Poppen created the first snowboard in Muskegon, Michigan. He nailed two old skis together, and he called his board a "snurfer." Around the same time in New Jersey, Tom Sims created his own snowboard. He redesigned his skateboard to ride on the snow.

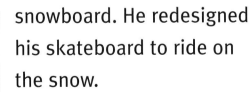

People's experiences with surfing, skiing, and skateboarding led to the development of snowboarding.

Dimitrije Milovich and Jake Burton Carpenter also created their own snowboard inventions in New York. As people traveled around the country with their new designs, snowboards became more popular.

By the 1970s, snowboards began to appear in magazines across the United States. Before long, snowboards were everywhere, and people could not wait to try them!

What's Your Game?

All snowboarding involves free-flowing movements, some speed, and *balance.* There are three different styles from which to choose:

Freestyle is fun for kids who like to do tricks and make up their own moves. Most freestyle moves were adapted from skateboarding. A lot of the language used by freestylers comes from skateboarding, too. Anyone who can skateboard will probably find freestyle easy to learn.

Freecarving is the style most *professional* racers choose. This style of snowboarding is sometimes called **Alpine.** It is designed for downhill riding and high speeds. Freecarving is not for beginners!

Freeriding is an all-purpose snowboarding style. It can be done in **backcountry** woods, in deep snow, or on mountaintops. Freeriding is easy and fun. Anyone with good balance can learn how to do it. Freeriding is a cross between freestyle and freecarving.

Ride Free!

There's a snowboard built for every snowboarding style!

Freestyle boards are short, light, and *flexible.* Some freestyle boards have the same shape along both sides and the two ends (also called tip and tail). This is called a twin tip. Twin tip boards have equal distance between the bindings and the tip and tail. (Bindings attach the boots to the board.) They have a **stomp pad** between the bindings for *traction.* Freestyle boards are built for soft boots. Two straps secure the boots to the board. A **leash** keeps the board attached to the snowboarder.

Freeriding boards are a little stiffer and wider than freestyle boards. The tip and tail of the board turn up slightly to help the board glide over the snow. Freeriding boards have a stomp pad, a leash, and a three-strap binding. These boards can go anywhere and are the easiest boards to use.

Freecarving boards are the stiffest, narrowest, and longest boards of all. The tail hardly turns up at all. Freecarving boards are built for high speed and smooth turns. Snowboarders wear hard boots. They use plate bindings to secure the hard boots to the board.

Freecarving board

Freestyle board

9

Suiting Up

What do riders wear when they are out in the snow all day? They wear lots of layers to keep them warm and dry. Most snowboarders wear three layers of clothing. Thermal underwear goes on closest to the body, and thick socks cover the feet. Next comes a wool or fleece sweater. Last comes the jacket and pants.

Outerwear keeps riders warm and dry. It should be windproof, waterproof, and made of "breathable" high-tech fabrics. It comes in many styles and bright colors. Snowboarders choose outerwear that expresses their personalities.

Snowboarders need additional equipment for safety.

Snowboarders wear waterproof gloves to protect their hands from the cold.

Boarders wear goggles and sunglasses to prevent glare and protect their eyes from the sun.

Snowboarders use sunscreen and lip balm to prevent sunburns during their long hours on the slopes.

Every snowboarder should wear a helmet and kneepads for safety. Helmets and kneepads protect boarders from injury when they fall.

Show Me How

If you are interested in snowboarding, lessons are a good way to begin. Snowboarding lessons are available for people of all ages and skill levels. You do not even need to know how to ski or skateboard before you learn how to snowboard. Beginning lessons might be as short as a few hours. To become an advanced rider, you probably will need several lessons. Ask about snowboarding lessons the next time you visit a ski resort with your family.

All lessons are taught by snowboarding instructors. Each instructor has a different way of teaching. Some like to explain things before they show how they are done. Others like to dive into action right away. All instructors will **demonstrate** moves before they let a beginner try them. The best instructors are **certified** by the American Association of Snowboard Instructors.

The best way to learn new skills is by taking a lesson and watching an instructor.

Talk the Talk

What does it mean when one snowboarder asks the other: "Did you see that sick fakie?" In snowboard speak, "sick" means totally awesome. A "fakie" is a backward move.

Snowboarders, or "boardheads," have their own special language. On the next page is a list of some cool words to know.

Marcel Hitz of Switzerland "shreds" his ride at the 2002 Salt Lake City Winter Olympic Games.

bail	to give up halfway through a move and fall
boned out	a straight-leg move
bonking	bouncing off objects on a slope
catching air	jumping through the air
dust on the crust	thin snow covering over ice
endo	falling face down into the snow
powder	deep snow
ride	a snowboard run down the slope
ripped	a perfectly executed move
shred	to have a great time, or to ride fast and with great style
sketch	to lose control on a snowboard
slam	crash
wheelie	a move done on the tip of the snowboard
wipeout	a really big fall

Goofy or Regular?

Goofy is more than just a character from Disney! It is also the way a snowboarder stands on a board. In the goofy position, a snowboarder's right foot is forward. In the regular position, snowboarders put their left foot forward. How do they know which foot goes first? They think about which foot they would stand on if they were kicking a ball. That would be the forward foot.

Standing up on a snowboard may feel awkward the first few times. Here's how you do it. Sit down in the snow. Strap your forward foot into the binding. Strap your rear foot in next. Then inch up close to the board. Use both of your hands to push up. Remember to place the board across the hill when you are standing up on a slope. Otherwise you will slide straight down the hill!

Everybody falls when they are learning to snowboard. Learning how to control a fall helps prevent snowboarding injuries. Try to relax and roll into the fall. Tuck in your head and hands when you fall. Never use your hands to break a fall.

Easy Does It

Pilots learning how to fly don't just jump into the cockpit and take off. They practice on the ground first. That's exactly how snowboarders do it.

All snowboarders should practice on a flat, **groomed** area. First practice **skating** with your front foot strapped onto the board. Use your free foot to push off. Keep the board flat and try skating forward. Then try skating in circles.

Next, try skating on a little hill. To get to the top, place your board across the hill and take small steps. The board should leave marks in the snow that look like stairs.

Julie Pomagalski of France edges a turn on her run at the 2003 FIS Snowboard World Championships.

Gliding on a small hill uses the same movement as skating. Rest your back foot on the board against the rear binding. Then balance your body above the center of the board, placing a little extra weight on your front foot. Don't look down! Keep your face forward to avoid running into something or someone!

Snowboarders naturally slow down and stop when they reach the flat area at the bottom of a hill.

Are You Ready?

All the exciting tricks that snowboarders perform begin with some very basic movements.

Edging describes the way a rider balances on the edges of a snowboard. Every snowboard has four edges. The front edge is called the toe. The rear edge is called the heel. The two long sides of the snowboard are the side edges. To tilt the board on the **toe edge,** lean forward a little and bend your knees. Rise up on your toes and hold the position for a few seconds. To tilt the board on the **heel edge,** lean backward a little. Lift your toes up and bend your knees to the side.

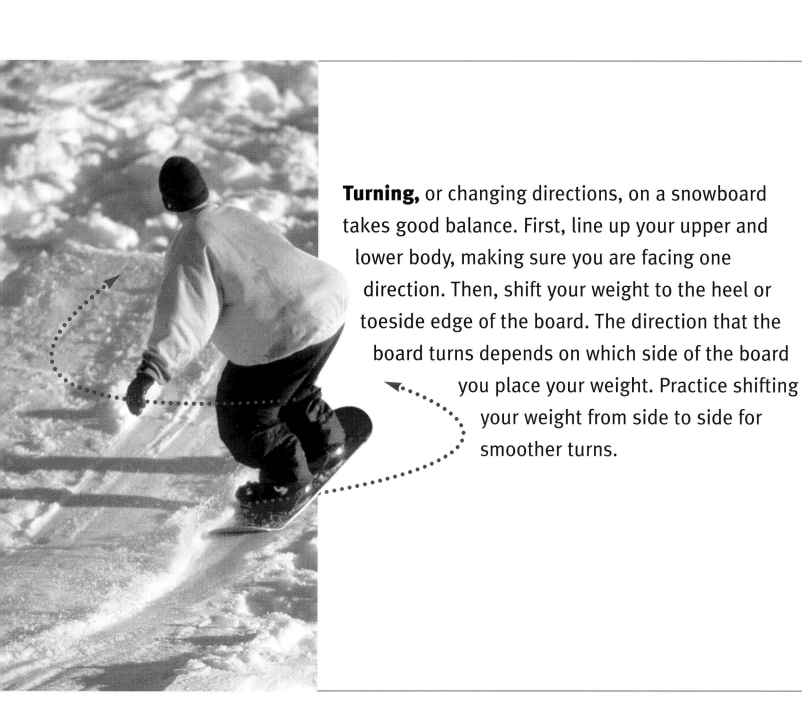

Turning, or changing directions, on a snowboard takes good balance. First, line up your upper and lower body, making sure you are facing one direction. Then, shift your weight to the heel or toeside edge of the board. The direction that the board turns depends on which side of the board you place your weight. Practice shifting your weight from side to side for smoother turns.

Stop and Go

Edging and turning (see p. 20–21) are the skills a snowboarder uses to control speed and direction.

The **J-turn** is one of the first turns a snowboarder learns. To make a J-turn, you start with a glide, but don't wait to reach the bottom to stop. Keep your free foot against the back binding and bend your knees. Then twist your body in the direction of the turn. Next, move your body in the opposite direction. Finally, lift your toes and tilt the board on the heel edge. When making a J-turn, snowboarders leave behind tracks in the snow that look like the letter "J."

This snowboarder is turning to finish off a J-turn.

Gliding across a hill is called traversing. Traversing helps snowboarders connect their turns. Begin by pointing your board across, not down, the hill. Then place your weight on your free foot. Keep the board on the toe edge and put the rear foot on the stomp pad. Next, ride the board all the way across the hill, lifting your toes to stop. Practice traversing on the toe and heel edges.

Putting It All Together

Once snowboarders have mastered the basic moves, they learn more difficult skills. Here are some of the most common intermediate-level moves that snowboarders use:

Sideslipping is a lot like traversing. Fasten your rear foot into the binding. Then place your board on its edge across the hill. Keep your weight evenly distributed. Next, slowly lower your heel edge toward the snow and slide sideways for a few seconds. Finally, lift the heel edge to stop.

The **falling leaf** is a reverse traverse. First glide across the hill on the toe edge of your board. Then shift your weight to the rear foot. Steer your board so that the heel edge is pointed downhill and keep the toe edge down. Now slowly glide in the opposite direction. Finally, ride backward and steer the board back across the top of the hill to stop. Practice on both the toe and heel edges of the board.

Garlands are a series of half turns down and across a hill. They make looping tracks in the snow that look like holiday decorations. A garland begins with a glide downhill on the toe edge of the board. To turn the board, twist your front leg in the direction you want to move. Next, flatten out the board and make a half turn. Then glide across the hill. Glide, turn half way, and traverse the hill three times.

Turning the front of the board back and forth will make garlands.

Cool Moves

Ready for some fun? Try these freestyle tricks.

Anyone who can do a falling leaf (see p. 24) can ride fakie. Keep your weight on the rear foot and steer the tail of your board downhill. Then change edges in the middle of the turn. Next, twist your front foot in the desired direction to steer the board all the way through the turn. Finally, twist your rear foot in the opposite direction.

Next, try an **Ollie.** Ride down the hill, bending your knees slightly. Then extend your arms outward and crouch down slowly. Next, place your weight on your rear foot to raise the toe of the board. Now, lift up off the snow with your toe-edge first and level the board out. The tighter the crouch, the higher the board will go. Finally, land on both of your feet. If you can hop from foot to foot and raise both your knees at the same time, you can do an Ollie!

Catching air is a little bit like flying. Practice on level ground first. Then spring straight up into the air. Land with your knees slightly bent. Try the same move over some **berms** or ledges in the snow. Keep your body centered over the board. Start with small jumps before you try big jumps.

Snowboarders practice "catching air" to increase their speed and height.

Ticket to Ride

What's the shortest way to the top of a mountain? It's a lift, of course.

Riding an **aerial lift** is like riding in a small subway car. Riders carry their boards on and off the car. They stand or sit as the car makes its way along a heavy cable up the mountain. Aerial lifts are easiest for beginners.

There are also two kinds of **surface lifts.** One has a handle that is attached to a moving cable. Snowboarders hold on to the handle as the cable tows them up the mountain. T-bars work the same way, except a bar goes behind the rider. It pushes the riders up the mountain instead of towing them. When riding a surface lift, snowboarders wear their boards. Only the front foot is strapped into the binding. The rear foot remains free and is used for balance. Snowboarders use the J-turn to get off a surface lift.

Chairlifts are seats or benches that carry a rider up the mountain. Riders strap one foot onto the board and keep the other foot free. There is usually someone to hold the chair while the rider gets on the lift. To get off a chair lift, snowboarders point the nose of their board straight ahead. Then, they place their back foot in the stomp pad and glide down the unloading ramp.

Both snowboarders and skiiers share chairlifts to travel up the mountain.

Perfect Powder

Not all snow is created equal! Different types of snow cover every slope. The type of snow that covers the slope affects a snowboarder's performance. Here are the most common types of snow and conditions:

Fresh powder is the snow that covers mountains and trees just after a storm. Fresh powder is the ultimate experience for most snowboarders because it is deep and unmarked by other riders. To enjoy fresh powder, snowboarders get up extra early and hit the slopes.

Light powder is the dusting of snow that covers groomed trails after a snow shower. Snowboards glide on top of light powder instead of riding in it. A fast ride is the best ride in light powder.

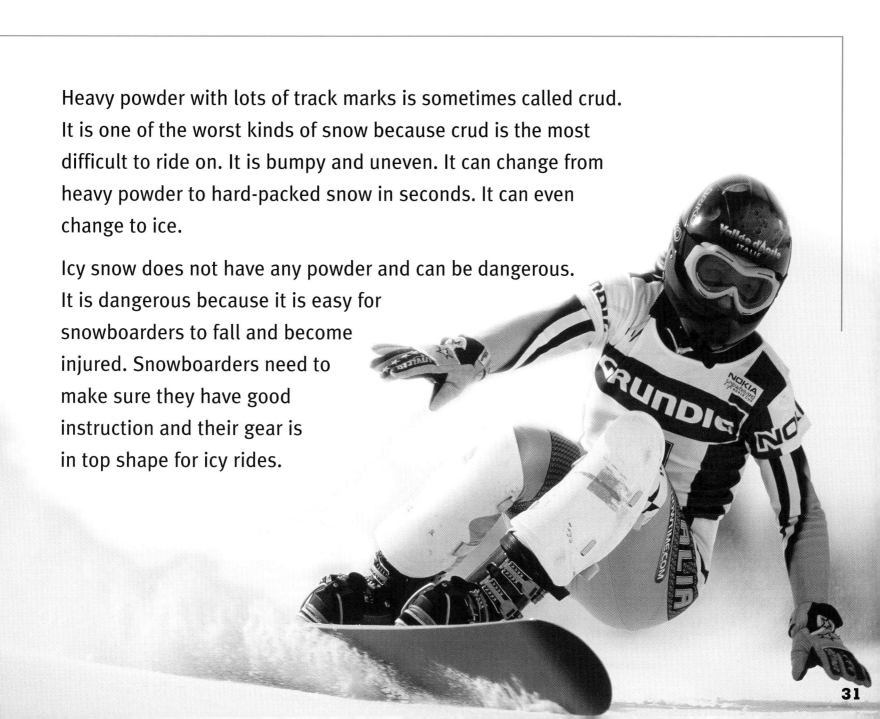

Heavy powder with lots of track marks is sometimes called crud. It is one of the worst kinds of snow because crud is the most difficult to ride on. It is bumpy and uneven. It can change from heavy powder to hard-packed snow in seconds. It can even change to ice.

Icy snow does not have any powder and can be dangerous. It is dangerous because it is easy for snowboarders to fall and become injured. Snowboarders need to make sure they have good instruction and their gear is in top shape for icy rides.

Know the Signs

Being prepared is the best way to make sure that every snowboard outing is a safe one.

All slopes have signs that tell snowboarders how steep and how difficult they are. Easy runs are marked with a green circle. Signs for intermediate runs have a blue square. Difficult runs are marked with a black diamond. Expert run signs have two black diamonds.

Signs also tell snowboarders about the conditions on a slope. Yellow and black poles warn that rocks, bumps, and holes are hidden under the snow. A black "X" on a yellow triangle indicates two slopes crossing.

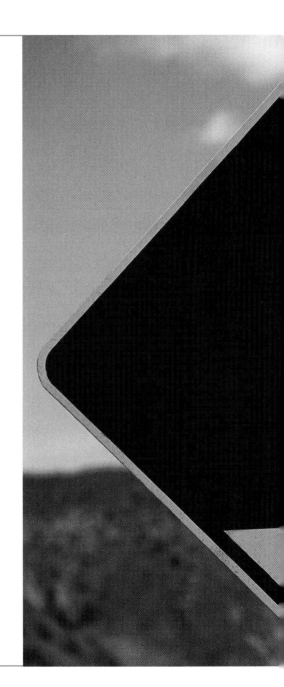

Snowboarders also have to understand the safety signals their own bodies are giving them. Numbness in the fingers or feet, dizziness, or sleepiness may be signs of **hypothermia.** Hypothermia is a serious condition caused by extreme cold, and it requires immediate medical attention. If not treated, hypothermia can be life threatening. Check the weather before snowboarding. Make sure you dress for the elements. Come in for some hot cocoa if you get too cold!

The Ones to Watch

Being a member of a snowboarding team is a great way to gain experience, try new equipment, and build confidence. Team members share tips and tricks with their teammates. They have a lot to talk about because they share the same interest—snowboarding!

There are teams for every age and ability. Young snowboarders might think about joining a local or *amateur* team. These teams offer good training and an opportunity to prepare for more advanced competitions.

Snowboard *manufacturers,* sports clubs, and other businesses *sponsor* teams for more experienced riders. These teams train just like professionals. They have coaches and wear uniforms. They also practice for the same kinds of events used in professional competitions. Top teams travel across town, across the state, and even across the country for competitions. They are the ones to watch for future stars who will make it to the really big competitions.

Take Your Marks

The biggest snowboarding competition is held every four years at the Winter Olympic Games. Snowboarding was first demonstrated at the 1994 Olympics. It became an official Olympic sport in 1998. In 2002, it was one of the most popular events in the Olympics at Salt Lake City, Utah. Two events were included.

In the parallel giant **slalom,** riders run on side-by-side courses with gates. Each competitor races one time on each course. The snowboarder with the fastest combined score for the two runs moves on to the next round.

The **halfpipe** is a freestyle event. Snowboarders speed down a ***cylinder***-shaped slope, then do tricks as they go over the rim. Riders are judged on technique, spins, height, landings, and the difficulty of their tricks.

All competitive racing consists of Alpine and freestyle events. Other exciting races to watch are the U.S. Open, the World Championships, the Grand Prix, and the Mount Baker Banked Slalom in Washington.

Pete Thorndike competes against Darren Ratcliffe in the dual slalom portion of the 2002 Snowboard Grand Prix.

On the Edge

Looking for a real thrill? Then tune into the Winter X-Games and Gravity Games for some of the most heart-stopping action ever seen on national TV! Here are some of the events included in these **extreme snowboarding** competitions:

There's lots of pushing and shoving in the **boardercross** event. Six riders race downhill at the same time. Each snowboarder must ride around *obstacles* placed on the course. To reach the finish line, they must fly over a huge gap. Speed is what counts in boardercross.

The **superpipe** is an event judged on style. Riders show off their sharpest and most difficult tricks. Twenty-four men and 24 women get three tries each to do their best. Watch for fantastic double **grabs** and upside-down spins.

Slopestyle competitions are fast and fun to watch. The course is covered with crazy obstacles like picnic tables and mailboxes. Riders are judged on how well they *navigate* the course. Judges also consider originality, style, technique, and height in a rider's score.

Big moves count in the **big air** competition. Riders come out hard and fast. They take off high into the air and perform spectacular moves. Then they try to **stick** their landing. Judges award points based on how high a rider goes, how far, the difficulty of the trick, and the landing.

Shaun White does an inverted grab during the 2003 Men's Snowboard Superpipe Competition at the X-Games VII.

Snowboard Superstars

Shaun Palmer

Some people call Shaun Palmer the bad boy of snowboarding. In the 1980s, his outrageous behavior made him a celebrity. But there was one thing he was serious about. That was snowboarding. Shaun was born in California in 1968. He started riding when he was 15, on a board he made himself. Shaun has won an incredible 15 World Championships! His favorite style of snowboarding is boardercross. He loves Frank Sinatra records, old Cadillac cars, and his mom.

Kelly Clark

For Kelly Clark, 2002 was a great year! She won three Grand Prix events, the Olympic halfpipe gold medal in Salt Lake City, and the U.S. Open quarterpipe and halfpipe. Kelly was born in Newport, Rhode Island, in 1983. She has been riding since the third grade and competing since she was 13. It is hard to predict what the future holds for Kelly, but you can bet it's going to be great!

What Happened When?

1778   **1900**   **1960**   **1965**   **1970**   **1975**   **1980**

1778 British explorer James Cook reports sightings of surfboarders in the Hawaiian islands.

1900s Children make the first skateboards by attaching roller skate wheels to planks of wood.

1920s Surfboarding catches on in Hawaii when Duke Paoa Kuhanamoku rides the waves on his red board.

1963 Tom Sims builds the first ski-board in his eighth-grade shop class.

1965 Sherman Poppen invents the snurfer board. Around the same time, Dimitrije Milovich and Jake Burton Carpenter come up with their own invention for riding on snow.

1968 The world's first "snurfer" contest is held on February 18, at Blockhouse Hill in Muskegon, Michigan.

1977 Jake Burton Carpenter designs the prototype for Burton Snowboards.

1979 Paul Graves dazzles the crowd at Blockhouse Hill with a freestyle demonstration.

1981 Competitive snowboarding gets off to a running start with a contest in Leadville, Colorado.

1982 Paul Graves organizes the first National Snowsurfing Championships in Woodstock, Vermont. It is the first time riders from all over the country compete.

1983 Jake Burton Carpenter launches the National Snowboarding Championships in Snow Valley, Vermont, and introduces his new snowboarding equipment. Tom Sims holds the first World Snowboarding Championships in Lake Tahoe, California. The halfpipe event makes its debut here.

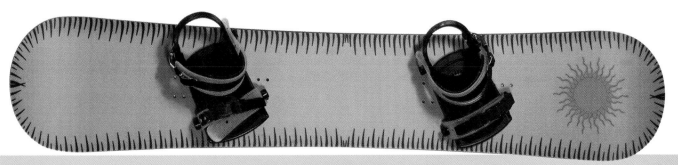

1985   **1990**   **1995**   **2000**

1985 Tom Sims wins the first annual Mount Baker Legendary Banked Slalom competition.

1987 The North American Snowboard Association (NASBA) is created. It uses the initials NASBA because NASA is already taken.

1987-1988 Two events in Europe and two events in the United States mark the first World Cup competitions.

1989 Most major ski resorts finally allow snowboarding on their slopes.

1990 The USASA holds the first annual national championships in Snow Valley, California. The International Snowboard Federation is formed.

1993 The first official Snowboard World Championships are held in Austria. The Federation Internationale du Ski (FIS) recognizes snowboarding as an official sport. The first World Extreme Snowboard Championships are held in Alaska.

1995 Organizers announce that snowboarding will be included at the 1998 Winter Olympic Games in Nagano, Japan.

1998 Snowboarding makes its debut at the XVIII Winter Olympics in Nagano, Japan, with parallel giant slalom and halfpipe competitions for men and women.

2002 Americans sweep the snowboarding events at the XIX Winter Olympics in Salt Lake City, Utah. Kelly Clark takes home the gold in the women's halfpipe. Danny Kass, Ross Powers, and J. J. Thomas each win medals for the men's halfpipe.

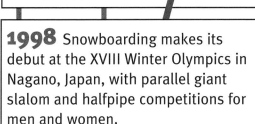

Snowboarding Fun Facts

Snowboard designs have come a long way. In 1979, Jake Burton Carpenter took his custom-made board to the annual snurfing competition in Muskegon, Michigan. He used large rubber bands to secure his feet to the board! Today his boards are world famous.

Tom Sims, a champion snowboarder and one of America's original snowboard creators, was the stunt double for actor Pierce Brosnan in the James Bond movie *A View to a Kill*.

Everyone was cheering for American Chris Klug (right) when he claimed a bronze medal in the men's parallel giant slalom event at the 2002 Winter Olympic Games. Just two years before, he received a liver transplant.

Today, snowboarding is more than a fad. Sales of snowboarding equipment in the United States alone are over $235 million.

Climbing Mount Everest, the world's tallest mountain, is hard enough. Stefan Gatt made history. He climbed to the top of Mt. Everest— and snowboarded down.

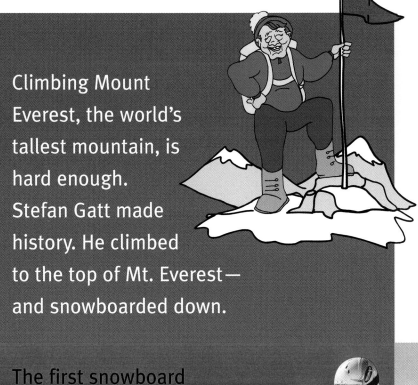

The first snowboard Dimitrije Milovich made weighed 45 pounds (20.4 kilograms). Imagine carrying that up a hill!

Stephen Koch has a dream. He wants to snowboard down the biggest mountains on the planet. He has already boarded down Mt. Aconcagua, Mt. McKinley, Kilimanjaro, Mt. El'brus, Vinson Massif, and a sky-high peak in New Guinea. Mt. Everest is next on his list.

Snowboarding Words to Know

aerial lift: a transportation system that carries snowboarders up a mountain in small cars, trams, or gondolas

Alpine: a style of snowboarding that involves downhill racing and high speeds

backcountry: any place away from groomed slopes and lifts

berm: a small ledge or jumping off point in the snow

big air: a high-flying event in extreme snowboarding competitions

boardercross: a downhill race with obstacles and jumps, seen at extreme snowboarding competitions

chairlift: a bench or seat attached to a cable that carries snowboarders up a mountain

edging: the manner in which a rider balances on a board to control speed and direction

extreme snowboarding: sporting competitions that involve daring risks, high speed, and fast action

falling leaf: a snowboarding move that involves crossing a hill in a backward direction

freestyle: a snowboarding style that involves original moves and tricks

grab: a freestyle move in which the rider holds on to a part of the board with the hand

groomed: a ski slope that has been cleaned and smoothed over

halfpipe: a U-shaped channel in the snow designed for aerial moves

heel edge: the edge of the snowboard on which the back of the foot, or heel, rests

hypothermia: a serious medical condition caused by extreme cold

J-turn: a beginner's turn used for stopping, which leaves marks in the snow that look like the letter "J"

leash: a cord that fastens a snowboard to the leg or foot of the rider

Ollie: a basic snowboarding trick or easy jump

outerwear: the top layer of clothing worn by a snowboarder, usually a jacket or parka and pants

sideslipping: a sideways sliding move on a snowboard

skating: a move used by snowboarders to travel across flat ground or up to a lift

slalom: a timed snowboard race in which riders move around gates and down a mountain

slopestyle: a downhill race with multiple obstacles, seen at extreme snowboarding competitions

stick: to land solidly with both feet on the snow and hold that position, without moving or wobbling

stomp pad: a rubber-covered rectangle on a snowboard, located between the bindings, that provides traction

superpipe: a halfpipe course designed for very high aerial moves

surface lift: a handle or T-bar attached to a cable that tows a rider up a mountain

toe edge: the edge of the board on which the front of the foot, or toes, rests

turning: a twisting move used by snowboarders to control speed and direction

Other Words to Know

Here are definitions for some of the words used in this book:

amateur: someone who competes in a sport as a hobby

balance: the art of holding the body in a difficult position

certified: a designation that shows an individual has passed specific tests

cylinder: the space created in the hollowed-out half of a tube-shaped object

demonstrate: to show or illustrate

flexible: the ability to bend or move easily

manufacturer: a person who makes a product for sale

navigate: to steer a course

obstacle: something that stands in the way of a person or thing

professional: a person paid to do a job or play a game

sponsor: a person or organization that pays for something another person does

traction: the grip created on a surface by body weight and movement

Where to Learn More

AT THE LIBRARY

Iguchi, Bryan. *The Young Snowboarder*. New York: Dorling Kindersley, 1997.

Layden, Joe. *No Limits: Burton Snowboards' Pro Riders*. New York: Scholastic, 2001.

Masoff, Joy. *Extreme Sports: Snowboard!* Washington, D.C.: National Geographic, 2002.

ON THE ROAD

Mt. Hood Snowboard Camp
P.O. Box 140
Rhododendron, Oregon 97049
800/247-5552
www.snowboardcamp.com

U.S. National Ski Hall of Fame and Museum
Box 191
Ishpemig, MI 49849
906/485-6323

Vermont Ski Museum
1 South Main St., The Perkins Building
Stowe, Vermont 05672
802/253-9911
www.vermontskimuseum.org

ON THE WEB

International Snowboard Federation of North America
www.snowboardranking.com

Snowboarding and Snowboard Life Magazines
www.snowboarding-online.com

United States of America Snowboard Association (USASA)
www.usasa.org

INDEX

ABOUT THE AUTHOR

Beth Gruber has written about, edited, and reviewed children's books for almost 20 years. She has also interviewed authors and TV show creators who write for children. Beth lives in New York City. She is a graduate of NYU School of Journalism. Reading and writing are her passion.